STRANGE
NOVA SCOTIA

VERNON OICKLE
ILLUSTRATED BY JULIE ANNE BABIN

MacIntyre Purcell Publishing Inc.
194 Hospital Rd.
Lunenburg, Nova Scotia
B0J 2C0
(902) 640-3350

www.macintyrepurcell.com
info@macintyrepurcell.com

Printed and bound in Canada by Marquis.

Cover Art: Kevin O'Reilly

Library and Archives Canada Cataloguing in Publication

Oickle, Vernon, 1961-, author   Strange Nova Scotia /
Vernon Oickle ; illustrated by Julie Anne Babin.

Issued in print and electronic formats. ISBN 978-1-927097-98-4 (paperback).--ISBN 978-1-77276-000-2 (html)

        1. Nova Scotia--Social life and customs--Caricatures and cartoons. 2. Canadian wit and humor, Pictorial (English). I. Babin, Julie Anne, illustrator II. Title.

FC2311.3.O43 2016   971.6   C2016-902190-4
                                                  C2016-902191-2

MacIntyre Purcell Publishing Inc. would like to acknowledge the financial support of the Government of Canada and the Nova Scotia Department of Tourism, Culture and Heritage.

FROM THE AUTHOR

I've often thought of Nova Scotia as a world unto itself. As one of the oldest places in Canada, the province is steeped in a rich and varied history, as its original Mi'kmaq people were joined by French Acadian settlers, British Loyalists, Scottish Highlanders, German and French Protestants, Irish peasants fleeing famine and later by Italian and Polish miners.

The province boasts many firsts, including the first responsible government (as opposed to British colonial government) in Canada, the first free press in Canada and the oldest university outside Britain in the former British Empire. Nova Scotians also have a rich maritime history having built the world's largest wooden ship and the North Atlantic's fastest fishing schooner.

In addition to the rich heritage, Nova Scotia also boasts a pristine environment with a variety of eco-systems and unspoiled natural spaces with jaw-dropping beauty that can rival any other place on earth. Beyond all of this, though, the province can also lay claim to some unusual and, yes, strange phenomena.

It is easy to see then that Nova Scotia is, indeed, a strange and wonderful place and I'm willing to bet that in this book, you will discover a collection of fun, intriguing and interesting facts that you didn't know about this wonderful province.

This book is truly a testament to Julie Anne Babin, my partner in this project. With her artistic abilities, she has somehow managed to capture the true essence and spirit of this place. We invite you, then, to take a journey into Strange Nova Scotia.

— Vernon Oickle

Dedicated to Julie Anne's mom,
Margaret Anne

AM I BLUE?

Nova Scotians have been called "Bluenoses" or "Bluenosers" since the 1700s because of the blue marks left on the noses of fishermen by their blue mitts. It's also the nickname given to the Nova Scotia British troops, which occupied New York City and Boston during the American Revolution.

FETCH ... OR NOT!

Adopted in 1995 by an Act of the House of Assembly, the Nova Scotia Duck Tolling Retriever is a purely Canadian breed. Originally bred as a "tolling" dog (one which lures game to the hunters rather than retrieving it), the Toller is the smallest of all Retrievers and is a medium sized breed of gun dog originating in Little River Harbour, Yarmouth County, around the beginning of the 19th Century.

DID I JUST SEE WHAT I THOUGHT I SAW?

During the War of 1812, an American Privateer called *The Young Teazer* was chased into Chester by a British ship and was trapped there. Rather than being captured, one of the crewmen tossed a flaming brand into the magazine hatch, blowing the ship to pieces. Only eight of the crew on board the ship were known to have survived the explosion. Over the years, there have been many reports of people seeing the ghost of *The Young Teazer* haunting the coast and exploding into a ball of fire.

SORRY, CHARLIE!

G-EBOG

The Town of Wedgeport was once known as the Sport Tuna Fishing Capital of the World and attracted such historical figures as President Franklin D. Roosevelt, Amelia Earhart, Michael and Helen Lerner, Zane Grey and Ernest Hemingway. Bluefins often weigh more than 750 pounds. The world-record fish was taken off Nova Scotia in 1979. It measured 13 feet in length and weighed 1,496 pounds.

KNOCK, KNOCK!

Alfred Fuller, who was born January 13, 1885, on an Annapolis Valley farm in Welsford, Kings County, made his mark on the world as the original "Fuller Brush Man." Eventually, he bought a home in Yarmouth.

DID YOU KNOW?

Samuel Mack was a wealthy entrepreneur who died at the age of 47 and was buried in the Old Port Medway Cemetery, Queens County, in 1783. Mack, who was one of the earliest settlers in the community founded one of the first lumber mills on the Port Medway River and was one of the early developers of nearby Bridgewater. A little-known fact is that he was also a great uncle to Joseph Smith, Jr., prophet and the founder of the modern Mormon religion.

ONE FOR THE RECORD BOOKS

Sister Anne Samson, who was born February 27, 1891, in River Bourgeois, Cape Breton, is believed to be the oldest Nova Scotian ever recorded. She lived a total of 113 years and 276 days. At the time of her death, on November 29, 2004, it was also believed that she was the oldest nun ever recorded in the world.

WHO IS THAT UNDER THERE?

The Unknown Comic is the stage name of actor and stand-up comic Murray Langston. Best known for his comic performances on *Rowan & Martin's Laugh-In*, *The Gong Show*, *Sonny and Cher* and *The Midnight Special*, he usually appeared on stage with a paper bag over his head. He wrote and acted in several movies, including the 1984 film *Night Patrol*. He was born in Dartmouth in 1945.

THAT'S A LOT OF SANDWICHES!

According to the Guinness Book of Records, the biggest lobster ever recorded weighed an amazing 20-kilograms (44 pounds) and was caught near Nova Scotia in 1977. From the tip of its tail to the tip of its claws it measured more than 110 cm. Now that's one big crustacean.

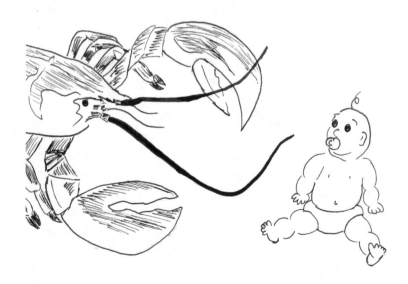

YUMMY IN MY TUMMY!

The traditional donair has origins in Greece, but the Halifax donair, complete with its trademark sweet sauce, was, as the legend goes, introduced in Halifax in the early 1970s. King of Donair founder, John Kamoulakos claims he developed the Maritime donair — a variation on the traditional Middle Eastern doner kebab — and first served up the now-popular meal at his restaurant on Quinpool Road in 1973.

THE ROCKETS

Robert Ross, born in 1766, was a British Army officer who is most well known for the burning of Washington, which included the destruction of the White House and United States Capitol in August 1814. This was retaliation for the destructive American raids into Canada, most notably the Americans' burning of York (Toronto), earlier in 1813.

His troops were met by the American Army at Bladensburg, fives miles north of Washington and Ross used Congreve rockets in the battle, which the Americans had never seen before. The British won the battle and marched into Washington where they set fire to a number of public buildings, including the president's mansion. The building was so badly stained with smoke that it had to be painted — white.

The following month, the British attempted to land at Baltimore, but were defeated. According to legend, a young lawyer named Francis Scott Key, after watching Ross' rockets red glare, was moved to compose a national anthem for his country to celebrate the sight of "the Stars and Stripes flying bravely in the dawn's early light to signal British defeat."

General Ross was killed at the Battle of North Point before the infamous Bombardment of Fort McHenry. His body was brought back to Halifax where it was buried in the Old Burying Ground on September 19, 1814 with full military honours. His grave is marked with a very formal, high, flat tombstone.

RED GLARE

WE ARE NOT ALONE!

In the tiny village of Shag Harbour on the night of October 4, 1967, shortly after 11 p.m., witnesses reported that a UFO, estimated at 60 feet in diameter, was seen hovering over the water. Those who saw the object reported that they saw four bright lights which flashed in a uniform pattern. After hovering for several minutes, witnesses said the object tilted and quickly descended toward the water. Witnesses, who immediately called the nearby RCMP detachment located in Barrington Passage, reported a bright flash that was followed by an explosion.

Neither the rescue co-ordination centre in Halifax nor the nearby NORAD radar facility at Baccaro had any knowledge

of missing aircraft, either civilian or military. Also, a coast guard lifeboat dispatched from nearby Clark's Harbour along with several local fishing boats were sent to the crash site, but the UFO had submerged before they reached the location. However, a sulfurous-smelling yellow foam was found bubbling to the surface from the point where the UFO went down. In a matter of time, a 120 by 300 foot slick developed.

The Shag Harbour UFO went on to became known as Case #34 in the infamous Condon Committee Report, but whatever the object was remains a mystery even today. This incident is the only UFO crash recorded and recognized by the Canadian Government.

SO, WHO REALLY **WAS** HERE FIRST?

Ever since 1812, when Dr. Richard Fletcher discovered the Runic (or Yarmouth) Stone on his property at the head of the Yarmouth Harbour, the Runic Stone has been the subject of academic and popular controversy. Many theories have been proposed as to the origin and content of the 13-character inscription on the face of the 400-pound stone. Although the nature of the mysterious inscription is still a matter of debate, the Norse rune theories remain the most persistent, thus giving the Yarmouth Stone its common name, the Runic Stone.

IN ONE DAY, YOU SAY?

The Church of Our Lady of Sorrows that stands in the Catholic cemetery in the south end of Halifax was erected by 200 parishioners in one day.

THE McKAY

In 1901, Nova Scotia became the first province in Canada to manufacture automobiles. Between 1911 and 1914, the Nova Scotia Carriage and Motor Company of Amherst produced about 100 cars called the McKay. The cars featured hand-buffed leather upholstery and an electric self-starter. The First World War and a shortage of operating capital cut off supplies, and the company folded.

STRIKE!

Canada's first lawn bowling green was built in the late 1880s at the Annapolis Royal garrison. In 1888, the country's first lawn bowling tournament was held in Toronto, and seven lawn bowling clubs competed, proving the game was growing in popularity.

FOR THE RECORD

The Casket in Antigonish is Canada's oldest continuing weekly newspaper. Its logo is a distinctive treasure chest from which the name was derived. *The Casket* started as a four-page newspaper in 1852.

THE FREE PRESS IS BORN

Canada's oldest daily newspaper and the third oldest in North America is the *Halifax Gazette*. The first issue of the *Halifax Gazette*, a half sheet with bits of news and some advertising, was published on March 23, 1752. The *Halifax Gazette* lives on today as the *Nova Scotia Royal Gazette*, official government publication for legal notices and proclamations.

IT'S A BIRD, IT'S A ...

John Alexander Douglas McCurdy (1886-1961) was the first person to fly an airplane in the British Empire when he piloted the *Silver Dart* at Baddeck in 1909. In 1910 he was the first Canadian issued a pilot's license and in 1911, he made the first flight from Florida to Cuba. He was the 19th Lieutenant-Governor of Nova Scotia from 1947-52 and established the first aviation school in Canada.

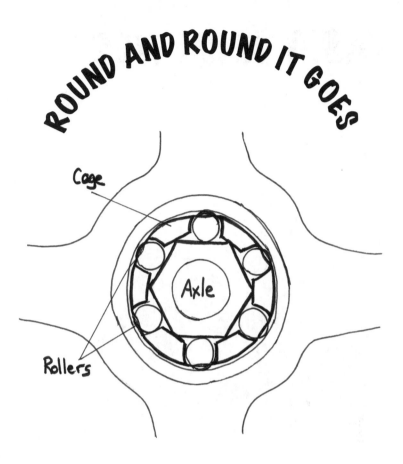

An innovation that has become invaluable to modern machine design was invented in 1879 at Bear River, Nova Scotia. George Welton Thomas wanted to eliminate or reduce the friction of moving parts against stationary ones such as a wheel revolving on an axle. Thomas achieved this with rollers in a cage, a design that continues to be used today in milling and factory machinery and just about everything that runs on wheels.

TASTY AND SWEET

James William Black from Berwick invented the ice-cream soda in 1886 when he created and bottled syrup made from whipped egg whites, sugar, water, lime juice or citric acid, flavouring extract and bicarbonate of soda. When ice water was stirred into a small ladle of the mixture it produced a delicious, foam-topped drink.

IF WE COULD TALK TO THE ANIMALS

The first zoo in North America was opened near Halifax
in 1847 by Andrew Downs, a world-famous naturalist
and taxidermist. His five-acre zoo had been in operation
for 12 years before the first American zoo was founded in
Philadelphia. Downs expanded his zoo to 100 acres and its
inhabitants became a favourite attraction for Halifax area
residents who arrived by steamboat.

ETCHED IN GLASS

St. Paul's Church, built in 1750, is the oldest Protestant church in Canada still standing. It is basically a simple wooden box with a peaked roof and steeple at one end. The church miraculously survived the Halifax explosion on December 6, 1917, but the story goes that its force blew a man through the Argyle Street window of the church. The silhouette was etched into the glass and no matter how many times the window is replaced the man's silhouette appears again.

THERE'S REAL FRUIT IN THERE

Do you enjoy your Raisin Bran or Apple Crisp flakes? If you do, you can thank George F. Humphrey of Bridgetown who, in 1924 and 1927, patented hot and cold breakfast foods infused with real fruit.

THE HIGH WATER MARK

LOW TIDE

LOWER TIDE

The highest tides on earth occur in the Minas Basin where the average tide range is 12 metres (38 feet), but can reach 17 metres (54.4 feet).

THAT SINKING FEELING

Nova Scotia can claim the questionable distinction of having more shipwrecks off its coast than any other province. By the end of the 20th Century, there were some 9,600 recorded wrecks off Nova Scotia, followed by Newfoundland with 7,000. Prince Edward Island had the least with 700, followed by New Brunswick with 1,800.

LOOK UP.
LOOK WAY UP!

The tallest person ever born in Nova Scotia was Anna Swan (1846-1888). She was born in Central near Tatamagouche in Colchester County and grew to the astounding height of 7 feet, 11 inches. Anna spent most of her life on stages around the world as P. T. Barnum billed her as the world's tallest person at a height of 8 feet, 1 inch. In England, she was presented to Queen Victoria and when sailing back to New York, she met another giant, Captain Martin VanBuren Bates of Kentucky, who was only one inch shorter than she was. When they were married in London, Queen Victoria presented Anna with a gold watch. When they left the circus circuit, Anna and Captain Bates moved to a custom-built house in Seville, Ohio. They had two children, both of which weighed over 20 pounds at birth, and both died in their infancy.

LIGHT THE WAY

Dr. Abraham Gesner (1797-1864) was born in Cornwallis, Nova Scotia, and was interested in nature, geology, mineralogy and chemistry. In 1864, he discovered kerosene by extracting oil from New Brunswick albertite. The clear, oily liquid had better illuminating properties than gasses currently in use at the time. He derived its original name "keroselain" from two Greek words meaning wax and oil. He first formed a company in Halifax to produce kerosene, and in 1853 moved to New York and set up two large factories for its production. He took out patent rights and sold them to the New York Kerosene Oil Works. The factories were soon overshadowed by E. L. Drake's discovery of large oil fields at Titusville, PA. Gesner's patent rights were challenged in the courts where he lost in biased judgments that ruled albertite was coal and his challengers had the licenses to mine coal and its minerals. He returned to Halifax to take the Chair of Natural History at Dalhousie University, but died before he could fill the post, having received none of the financial rewards for his invention.

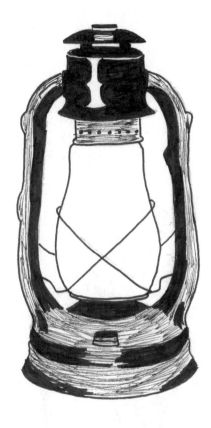

ON THE ICE

John Forbes of Dartmouth invented the clip-on skate in 1867. Instead of screws and plates to attach the blade to the boots of the wearer, Forbes' invention required only a single lever. Forbes came up with the idea while he was foreman at the Starr Manufacturing Company. More than 30 different kinds of skates were patented by Nova Scotia and New Brunswick inventors between 1867 and 1933.

A BRIDGE TOO FAR

When European newcomers suggested that a bridge linking
Halifax and Dartmouth would make life a lot simpler, a
Mi'kmaq chief warned that this would not be a good idea. He
said to build such a bridge would result in three failures — the
first would take place during a great wind; the second would
happen during a great quiet; and the third catastrophe would
result in great death. In 1887, a hurricane caused the collapse
of a railway bridge that had been built across the harbour. The
temporary bridge to replace the railway bridge fell down on
a calm and quiet night. The Angus L. Macdonald Bridge has
now been operating for more than half a century. What fate
awaits this existing link is unknown.

ON THE ROCKS

Such a fine Single-Malt Not Scotch!

Glenora Distillery at Glenville, located between Mabou and Inverness, is Canada's only single-malt distillery. Because it is not distilled in Scotland, the whiskey cannot be called "Scotch."

GOOD KNIGHT!

Sir Thompson, we are not amused!

Prime Minster John Thompson (1845-1894) of Halifax, died on his 50th birthday, November 10, 1894, from a sudden stroke during lunch at Windsor Castle, after being knighted that morning by Queen Victoria.

NOW THAT'S A TONGUE

Charles L. Grant of Grand Pré invented the gum rubber shoe in 1920. His innovation was a rubber-coated tongue fastened to the shoe, making it waterproof. His invention is now standard practice in shoe manufacturing.

OH CHRISTMAS TREE!

Nova Scotia was home to Canada's first decorated Christmas tree in 1846. The first time evergreen was used as a Christmas tree was in Sorel, Quebec in 1781, where German Baroness Riedsel made her own three children happy and made history by erecting the first Christmas tree on the continent.

WILL THAT BE TEA OR COFFEE?

In 1909, James Rooney invented a tea and coffee pot whose design is still in use today. It's a perforated receptacle with a plunger, which fits inside a tea or coffee pot letting leaves or grounds be easily removed after infusion.

GOING IN REVERSE

James A. Ross of Halifax is responsible for the backup lights on your automobile. Back in 1919, Ross realized the importance of such a device and connected the light to a switch on the gearshift lever and by doing so, lit the way for all future drivers.

WHAT COMES BETWEEN 4 AND 6?

The first reported quintuplets in Canada were born in Little Egypt, Pictou County in 1880. The three girls and two boys all died within two days.

In 1854, when Samuel McKeen of Mabou, Cape Breton, arranged a series of cogged gears to record the distance travelled by a wheel, which in those days was a carriage wheel, he was actually inventing the odometer. He took it a step further by adding a hammer and bell so the carriage passenger could hear as each mile marker was passed.

NOT SO TALL

The Prince of Wales Tower was built between 1796 and 1797 and was the first of its kind in North America. Edward, Duke of Kent, ordered the tower built on high ground behind Point Pleasant to defend batteries on Pleasant Point in Halifax, located to prevent enemy ships from entering the harbour. The Martello tower, named for Edward's older brother, is round, built of stone and is almost three times as wide as it is tall. There were six mounted guns on the roof and four on the second story. Today it is a national historic site.

FOGGED UP!

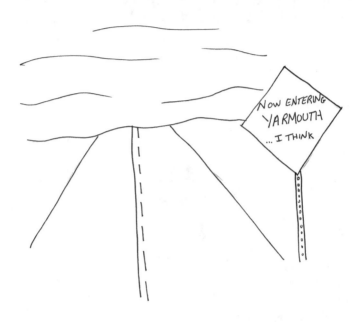

The longest stretch of fog ever recorded in Nova Scotia was 85 days in the summer of 1967 in Yarmouth. There were only seven days that summer when Yarmouth was fog-free.

PROPELLED INTO HISTORY

John Patch of Yarmouth invented a boat propeller in 1833 and demonstrated it on a small boat in Yarmouth Harbour. Because Nova Scotia's patent system was just getting started, Patch went to Washington, D.C. where his application was denied because he did not have a U.S. address. In 1849, he invented the "double-action propeller" and, armed with a Boston address, was able to patent it. However, by this time, his original invention was being claimed by American and European inventors and as a result, Patch received no compensation for his invention. He died a poor man.

LET'S IRON THIS OUT

John B. Porter of Yarmouth patented the portable ironing board in 1875. Today, it is the standard design of all ironing boards.

WHATEVER HAPPENED TO JOSHUA SLOCUM?

The fifth of 11 children born to a Quaker family, Captain Joshua Slocum (1844-1909) lived his boyhood years in Westport. He ran away from his disciplinarian father at age 12 to work as a cabin boy on a fisherman's ship. At 16 he made his first trip across the Atlantic and by 25, was in charge of a large schooner operating between San Francisco and Seattle. He is best known for being the first person to solo circumnavigate the globe, which he did between 1895 and 1898 in an 11.3 metre, (36-foot) sloop-rigged, former fishing boat named *Spray*. In 1909, he set sail for South America and was never heard from again, leaving the manner of his death a complete mystery.

SLITHERY STUFF

A rare breed of snake is found only on two small islands in Halifax Harbour. Wildlife experts have determined that the unusual looking black snakes are actually ordinary garter snakes and that their black pigmentation is a genetic aberration caused in part by inbreeding.

HIS NAME WAS JEROME

In 1863, a man was discovered on the beach at Sandy Cove near Digby. Both of his legs had been professionally amputated above the knees, were bandaged and only partially healed. Beside him were a jug of water and a tin of biscuits. A ship had been spotted offshore the previous day, so it was assumed he had been brought ashore after dark. Only the word "Jerome" could be determined from the man's moaning and muttering and it was presumed that was his name. For the next 49 years, Jerome never broke his silence, fuelling all sorts of speculation as to his origins and leading to his label – Mystery Man of Sandy Cove. He lived out his silent life with several local families, supported in part by a $2 weekly supplement from the provincial government.

BUCKLE UP!

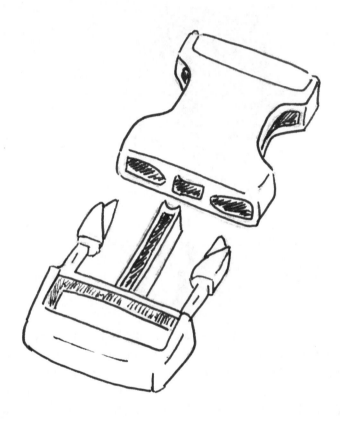

Each time you buckle up your seatbelt or snap closed a carry case, you can thank inventor Arthur Davy of New Glasgow. Seatbelts weren't what Davy had in mind when he invented the quick-release buckle in 1911. His idea was to simplify attaching and detaching the reins from a horse.

WINNING LOGO

The famous logo of a girl wearing a white bonnet on the Old Dutch Cleanser cans was designed by Maude E. Sutherland, daughter of a Pictou doctor. In 1907, the company ran a continent-wide logo contest and young Maude was the winner.

I PROMISE THAT I WILL DO MY BEST

North America's first Boy Scout troop was organized in Port Morien, Nova Scotia, in 1908, just a year after Lord Baden Powell began England's scouting movement. William Glover, an official at one of the coalmines, officially organized a troop of ten boys.

SHEEP OVERBOARD!

The fishing village of Port Mouton in Queens County was named "sheep port" by French explorer Du Gua de Monts in 1604 after a sheep jumped overboard and nearly drowned. Luckily for the sheep, the crew saved it, but they subsequently ate the waterlogged animal.

NO BONES ABOUT IT!

In 1985, the largest fossil find ever in North America was unearthed on the north shore of the Minas Basin near Parrsboro. More than 100,000 fossil specimens, some more than 200 million years old, were found, including penny-sized footprints. In 1984, collector Eldon George found the world's smallest dinosaur tracks at Wasson's Bluff.

THE BIGGEST, EVER!

The *W.D. Lawrence*, the largest square-rigger ever built in Nova Scotia and the largest wooden ship ever built in Canada, was launched at Maitland in 1874 by W.D. Lawrence.

FIDDLE MUSIC

Prince Edward Island once claimed the World's Largest
Fiddle, but Nova Scotia now makes that claim. Prince Edward
Island's fiddle at Cavendish is 7.3 metres (23.3 feet) high,
but the one at Sydney is 16.8 metres (53.7 feet) tall. The Big
Ceilidh Fiddle is owned by the Sydney Ports Commission.

SHIFTING SANDS

Sable Island is a long, narrow sandbar — 34 km long and
1.5 km wide — that's the highest point on the Continental
Shelf running under the Atlantic Ocean off the east coast. It's
also called the Graveyard of the Atlantic because there have
been hundreds of shipwrecks there with an estimated loss of
10,000 lives. The first reported wreck was in 1583 when the
shoals surrounding the island claimed one of Sir Humphrey
Gilbert's ships. In the late 1700s, 60 horses were shipped to
the island. Their descendants, now numbering about 250, still
look like rugged horses of centuries ago. A solar-powered
lighthouse now warns ships about the island.

MY, WHAT
BIG
HANDS
YOU HAVE!

The world's tallest genetically normal giant may have been born in the Hebrides of Scotland, but he moved to St. Anns, Cape Breton, when he was a child. Angus McAskill (1825-1863) was of normal size at birth, but by the time he was in his 20s, he was 2.36 metres (7.55 feet) tall and weighed more than 190 kg (418 pounds). McAskill's hands measured 20 by 30 cm (8 by 12 inches). While not in the circus, he did tour for a few years with a sideshow in which he demonstrated astonishing feats of strength. He eventually returned to Cape Breton in 1853 and ran a business.

EIGHT BALL IN THE CORNER POCKET!

The replaceable pool cue tip was patented in 1920 by George W. Leadbetter of Springhill. His metal sleeve has now been replaced by plastic and the tip is glued on, but Leadbetter's invention is credited with forever changing the construction of pool and billiard cues.

ONLY THE SHADOW KNOWS!

SAM

Shubenacadie Sam is North America's first prognosticator of whether or not we'll have to endure another six weeks of winter. That's because Sam is in the eastern time zone and makes his predictions before Punxutawney Phil, Wiarton Willie and other members of his family are up and about. Sam is a groundhog or woodchuck, and the legend of shadow-forecasting goes back to the 18th Century when Germans sought answers from hedgehogs. Settlers brought the tradition to Pennsylvania (home of Phil) and North Americans found groundhog shadows just as reliable. The tradition goes that if Sam sees his shadow on February 2 at Shubenacadie Provincial Park where he lives and scampers back into his burrow, Nova Scotians know they're in for six more weeks of winter weather.

Oxford claims to be the Blueberry Capital of the World. It also boasts the world's largest blueberry, which is located at a gas station. The incredible giant is 2.4 metres (7.5 feet) tall.

THE "REAL" STANFIELDS

What came to be known as "long johns" were invented
in Truro in 1915, and were originally called "underwear
combinations." Essentially, they were long underwear in two
pieces that could be adjusted to fit different body lengths.
Frank Stanfield came up with the idea in 1898. He and
his brother John had developed "Stanfield's Unshrinkable
Underwear" and they caught on.

BUG OFF!

In 1959, Charles Coll of Truro invented the mosquito repellent Muskol. Its magical ingredient is the chemical DEET.

SOMETHING FISHY

A staple in homes today, the frozen fish fillet was invented in Halifax in 1926 by Walter H. Boutilier and Frank W. Bryce. Sometime around 1940, they patented a process that allowed them to impregnate raw fish with a flavouring substance before freezing it.

TO TURN A PHRASE

Thomas Chandler Haliburton (1796-1865) was a lawyer, politician and judge born in Windsor, but he is best remembered as a writer and creator of the literary character, Sam Slick. In the mid-1830s, Haliburton wrote satiric sketches for the *Novascotian*, which were eventually collected into a book titled *The Clockmaker*. He had two sons and five daughters but none of them had children. In 1856, he moved to Great Britain, sat in the British Parliament and continued writing Sam Slick books. Some of the modern expressions that we continue to use today came from these books such as it's raining cats and dogs; honesty is the best policy; the early bird catches the worm; an ounce of prevention is worth a pound of cure; and jack of all trades and master of none.

N°. 1

The first license plate issued in Nova Scotia went to William Black of Wolfville on May 8, 1907 for an Oldsmobile Touring Car. The second was issued to Mr. W.L. Kane of Halifax. The plates had large black numbers on a white background along with the letters NS. In total, 62 license plates were issued that year. However, number 13 was not issued.

FLOWER POWER

Nova Scotia's official flower, the mayflower, symbolizes the province's ability to endure a harsh winter and return each spring. Also known as trailing arbutus, the mayflower was adopted by the legislature in 1901.

FULLY LOADED

Wine Harbour, located in Guysborough County, gets its name after a Portuguese barque loaded with casks of wine was wrecked here before 1818.

ORANGE GIANTS

Giant pumpkin growers around the world know the name Howard W. Dill (1934-2008) of Windsor. He sent the pumpkin-growing world into a tizzy in 1979 when he won the International Pumpkin Association weigh-off with a 438-pound (199 kilo) giant. But Dill wasn't content with that victory. He kept growing bigger and bigger pumpkins and winning more titles. He also sold seeds from his giants and eventually the great-great-grandchildren of his own pumpkins defeated him in world competition.

THE SULTAN OF SWAT

George Herman "Babe" Ruth was born on February 26, 1895, and went on to become one of the best major league baseball players of all time. During two seasons — 1920 and 1927— he hit more home runs (114) than any entire team in the American league, a feat never repeated again by any other player. While his exploits on the baseball diamond are the stuff of legend, "The Sultan of Swat" made many hunting and fishing trips to the Yarmouth area during the early part of the previous century. Ruth, guided by famed local Acadian-French outdoorsmen, Peter and Louis Vacon, was said to have made Tusket one of his favourite destinations and stories were told about his exploits throughout the province.

ENDANGERED SPECIES

Shelburne County has the highest concentration of plover beaches in the entire province. The Piping Plover is a small bird with a large, rounded head, a short, thick neck and a stubby bill. It is a sand-coloured, dull gray/khaki, sparrow-sized shorebird. The adult has yellow-orange legs, a black band across the forehead from eye to eye, and a black ring around the neck during the breeding season. The species is threatened and endangered globally. In Eastern Canada, the Piping Plover is found only on coastal beaches. In 1985, it was declared an endangered species by the Committee on the Status of Endangered Wildlife in Canada.

IF THESE WALLS COULD TALK

Oh, if these windows could talk!

The deGannes-Cosby house located at 477 St. George Street, Annapolis Royal is the oldest documented wooden structure in Nova Scotia and has been continuously occupied since its construction in 1708. It was built by Major Louis deGannes de Falaise — a native of France who was posted to Port Royal in 1696 — on the site of his previous house, which had burned in the unsuccessful siege of the town in 1707. Using the cellar foundation and both standing chimneys, he raised a post and beam frame and filled the walls with wattle and daub. In 1710, Port Royal changed hands for the final time and was renamed Annapolis Royal in honour of the reigning Queen. Two years later, the deGannes family returned to France.

Throughout most of the 18th century, the house was the home of the Cosby family, beginning with Alexander Cosby, who came to Nova Scotia in 1721 as a major in the 40th Regiment, commanded by his brother-in-law Richard Phipps, governor of the province. The deGannes-Cosby house is a provincially and municipally designated heritage building. It has had 16 owners in nearly 300 years and remains a private residence.

ANNA AND THE KING

Anna Harriette (Edwards) Leonowens was born November 6, 1831, in Ahmandnagar, India. A British subject, she was a travel writer, educator and social activist. She is best known for her experiences in Siam (Thailand) that were fictionalized in Margaret Landon's 1944 best-selling novel *Anna and the King of Siam*, as well as films and television series based on the book, most notably Rodgers and Hammerstein's 1951 hit musical *The King and I*.

During the course of her life, Leonowens also lived in Aden, Australia, Singapore, the United States and

N·S·C·A·D

Canada, more specifically Halifax and Montreal. In 1878, Leonowens's daughter, Avis Annie Crawford Connybeare married Thomas Fyshe, a Scottish banker and the general manager of the Bank of Nova Scotia in Halifax. Leonowens followed her daughter to Halifax where she settled and again became involved in women's education. She was a suffragette and one of the founders of the Local Council of Women of Halifax and the Nova Scotia College of Art and Design. After nineteen years, she moved to Montreal where she died on January 19, 1915, at the age of 83.

A **REAL FISH** STORY

The world's biggest Atlantic Bluefin Tuna ever recorded was caught by Ken Fraser in Aulds Cove, Nova Scotia on October 26, 1979. He landed the 1,496-pound (679 kilograms) fish in an impressive 45 minutes.

The Atlantic bluefin tuna is one of the largest, fastest and most beautifully coloured of all the world's fish. Their torpedo-shaped, streamlined bodies are built for speed and endurance. Their colouring — metallic blue on top and shimmering silver-white on the bottom — helps camouflage them from above and below. And their voracious appetite and varied diet pushes their average size to a whopping 6.5 feet (two meters) in length and 550 pounds (250 kilograms), although much larger specimens are not uncommon. They are among the most ambitiously migratory of all fish, and some tagged specimens have been tracked swimming from North American to European waters several times a year.

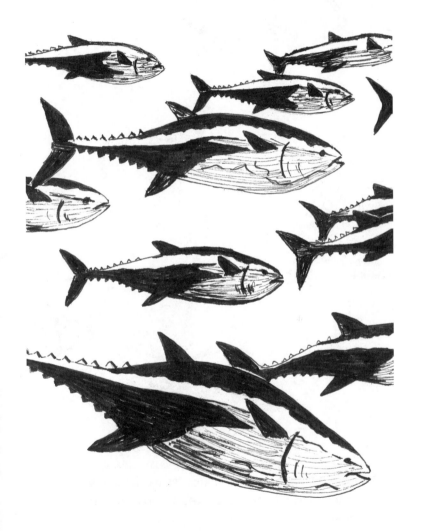

DID SOMEONE SAY JAWS?

In August 2004, while a local man was participating in the annual shark derby in the waters off the coast of Yarmouth, he ended up making a catch that was one for the record books.

Fishing with a rod and reel, using a 200-pound test line and a hook baited with mackerel, and chumming 48 miles out

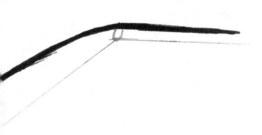

of Yarmouth, it wasn't long until he felt the bite. He knew right away it was a big one. He worked it for 30 minutes before he saw the fin, rising a good foot from the water about 150 yards out. It was a short fin mako shark. A regular visitor to Maritime waters, the sharks are often reported chasing mackerel with the Gulf Stream into the Bay of Fundy.

When they finally got it on the official scale, lifted into place by a forklift to keep the scale from tipping, the shark weighed in at an astonishing 1,082 pounds — a Canadian record and one of the largest ever caught. The female shark measured 10 feet, 11 inches in length and was estimated to be about 25 years old.

MUTINY
ON THE
BOUNTY

Bounty was an enlarged reconstruction of the original 1787 Royal Navy sailing ship HMS Bounty. Built in Lunenburg in 1960, she was commissioned by the Metro-Goldwyn-Mayer film studio for the 1962 film *Mutiny on the Bounty,* starring Marlon Brando and Trevor Howard.

Based on the novel *Mutiny on the Bounty* by Charles Nordhoff and James Norman Hall, the film retells the 1789 real-life mutiny aboard *HMAV Bounty,* led by Fletcher Christian against the ship's captain, William Bligh.

Bounty was the first large vessel built from scratch for a film using historical sources. Previous film vessels were fanciful conversions of existing vessels. More than 200 workers built the replica to the original ship's drawings from files in the British Admiralty archives over an eight-month period at the historic Smith and Rhuland shipyard, the same shipyard where the famous schooner *Bluenose* was built.

Sadly, she sank off the coast of North Carolina during Hurricane Sandy on October 29, 2012.

MOLLY KOOL

Born in the small community of Alma, New Brunswick
on February 23, 1916, Myrtle "Molly" Kool was North
America's first registered female sea captain or shipmaster.
She was the daughter of Myrtle Anderson and Paul Kool,
a Dutch sailor.

She grew up sailing, eventually becoming captain of
the Jean K, a 21-metre scow owned by her father. At 21,
she joined the Merchant Marine School in Saint John, New
Brunswick. She was the only woman to do so. Two years later
she graduated and received her Master Mariner's papers from
the Merchant Marine Institution in Yarmouth. As a result, a
line in the Canadian Shipping Act had to be amended to read
"he or she."

RIDE THE WIND

Canada's most famous sailing vessel, *Bluenose*, built in Lunenburg and launched on March 26, 1921, successfully raced against American competition for the International Fishermen's Trophy for 17 years, never having lost a race. Her namesake, *Bluenose II*, was launched on July 24, 1963, and the third incarnation of the vessel, also named *Bluenose II*, hit the waters of Lunenburg harbour September 29, 2012. The Duke of Devonshire, Governor General of Canada, drove a golden spike into the keel of *Bluenose* in December 1920 to mark the beginning of the historic vessel's construction.

THE MASTER MAGICIAN

Most Nova Scotians may not know this, but Harry Houdini, the famous escape artist, actually gave his first performance outside of the United States in Yarmouth. It was in May, 1896 when Houdini strolled along Yarmouth's Main Street before stopping in front of a hardware store. Stepping inside Scott's Bazaar, which sold wallpaper and other notions, he was soon performing his first amazing escape act on foreign soil as folks gathered around him. Customers watched as Houdini escaped from locked handcuffs, which he had brought with him.

The performance was going well when two Yarmouth cops, walking the beat, entered the store. One of them, policeman Harris Palmer, slapped his own handcuffs on Houdini and suggested he try to get out of them, which Houdini promptly did. Palmer was the very first policeman outside of America to handcuff Houdini.

In addition to the Yarmouth shows, it's recorded that Houdini did his first jail break at Halifax City Hall, where the police station used to be, and his performance in Dartmouth was actually his first performance outside of the United States as a headliner. Houdini, whose real name was Ehrich Weisz, died in Detroit at the age of 52 on October 31, 1926. He was buried in Machpelah Cemetery in Queens, New York.

RINK RATS

Canada's first permanent covered skating rink opened in
Halifax on January 3, 1863, as a private club — the Halifax
Skating Rink.

WE'RE OUTTA HERE ... WELL ALMOST

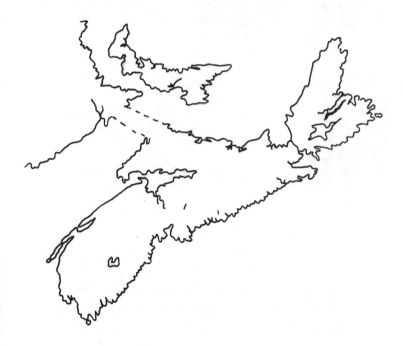

On January 12, 1868, Nova Scotia voted to leave
Confederation unless it got better terms.

THAT'S DEEP, MAN!
REAL DEEP

The 1,280-metre Canso Causeway, linking Cape Breton Island to Nova Scotia mainland, opened on December 10, 1954. It is the deepest causeway in the world.

IT'S
IN
THE
MAIL

Canada's first post office opened in Halifax on December 9, 1755, with subsidized direct mail to Britain. Nova Scotia issued its first stamp on September 1, 1851.

I'LL DRINK TO THAT!

Nova Scotia ended prohibition in favour of government control of liquor on October 30, 1929.

THE OLDEST IN THE LAND

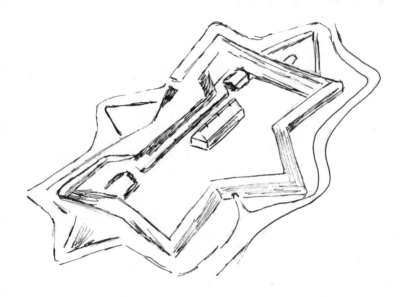

Fort Anne in Annapolis Royal became Canada's first National Historic Park in October 1917. Fort Anne is the oldest National Historic site in Canada. The key to Fort Anne, that had been taken to Boston in 1710, was finally returned to its original home in August 1922.

TILL DEATH ...
OR DIVORCE
DO US PART

Honourable Edward Cornwallis granted the first divorce in British North America in Nova Scotia. The year was 1750, a hundred years before the British House of Commons passed legislation of this kind for England.

PLUGGED

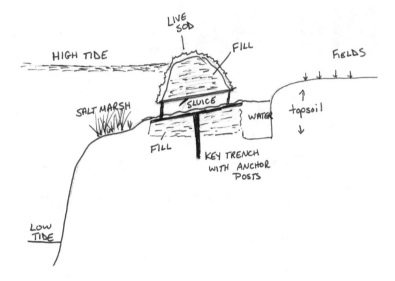

The first dyke in North America was built in 1710 in Annapolis.

NEITHER RAIN, NOR SLEET, NOR HAIL ...

In 1849, before the telegraph lines were finished to Halifax, men on horseback carried the mail throughout the province. This service was called the Pony Express.

UP IN SMOKE

The first crime of arson reported in Nova Scotia was committed in 1737 in Annapolis Royal by a servant of Lieutenant Amhurst. The servant set fire to his masters' house, which was completely destroyed. This was a capital offence in which the council had only silent instructions, so the offender got off.

HOLY WATER

The first regular Roman Catholic priest at Port Royal was Rev. Jesse Flesche, who accompanied Poutrincourt from France in February, 1610. He performed the first baptism in Canada on St. John's Day, June 24, 1610.

THE OLDEST IN THE LAND

Goat Island Baptist Church in Nova Scotia is the oldest
Baptist church building in Canada. It was built in 1810.

THE WHIPPING TREE

In July 1937, the large trunk of the willow tree known as "The Whipping Tree" in Annapolis Royal collapsed and had to be removed. The ancient tree had stood on the boundary line between the old cemetery and the Court House Square close to the sidewalk. It received its name from the tradition that prisoners sentenced to be lashed were fastened to its trunk to receive punishment.

EARLY LANDING

Possible landing of Prince Henry Sinclair was recorded at
Chedabucto Bay on June 2, 1398.

A STREETCAR NAMED ...

Yarmouth was the first town in the Maritimes to have its own electric streetcar service. It ran from Yarmouth South to Milton on a regular daily schedule, from August 1892 until October 1928.

IS THERE LIFE OUT THERE?

The first North American documented sighting of a UFO was on October 12, 1786, at New Minas.

PRESIDENTIAL VISIT

John Quincy Adams, former president of the United States, visited an old family friend in Halifax in 1840.

OH, ADELE!

Adele Hugo, daughter of world famous Victor Hugo fled to Halifax where she lived from 1863 to 1866, creating one of the 19th centuries most notorious love scandals.

THE
GENIUS

Oscar Wilde declared "his genius" as his only item of value
he was bringing to North America, when he went through
Halifax customs in 1882.

THE LUCKY PRINCE

LIFE ON THE SEA
IS NOT MY CUP OF TEA...
... I THINK I WILL BE
KING INSTEAD!

Prince George (future King George V) was saved from
drowning in Nova Scotia in 1883.

HIGH ON A HILL

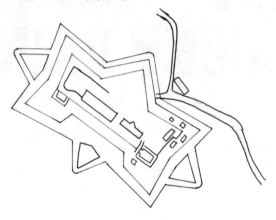

Benedict Arnold's son, Colonel Arnold, designed the initial plans for Halifax's famous Citadel Fort in 1818. Educated in Nova Scotia, he won fame in Egypt fighting against Napoleon.

COOL SHOPPING

The Halifax Shopping Center was North America's second air-conditioned shopping mall, after the Yorkdale Mall in Toronto, 1962.

BLOSSOM TIME

Royal Doulton's famous dinner pattern "Blossom Time"
depicts the famous May blossoms of the Annapolis Valley.

SPY MISSION

On July 4, 1936, the German airship Hindenburg flew over Nova Scotia at an altitude of about 1,000 feet, possibly taking pictures for German intelligence.

CHEW, CHEW, CHEW

For decades, Spruce Gum, a natural product of the forest of Nova Scotia, was sold internationally as a chewing gum.

PLACES WITH DISTINCTION

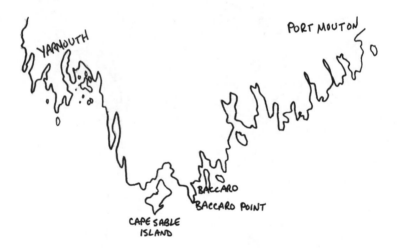

Baccaro, Shelburne County, is the oldest place name in Nova Scotia. It comes from the Basque word, Baccolaos for codfish. Baccaro Point in Shelburne County is the most southerly point of mainland Nova Scotia. Cape Sable Island, near Barrington Passage, is the most southerly point in Atlantic Canada.

BIG
FISH

The largest chain pickerel ever recorded in Canada was caught in Doctor's Lake, Yarmouth County in 1989. It weighed 2.44 kg (5.38 lbs).

FUNNY MONEY

Three pieces of Canadian currency depict images synonymous with the South Shore:

Bluenose first appeared on the dime in 1937, the Lunenburg waterfront was featured on the old Canadian $100 bill and Crescent Beach, a 1.5 kilometer of sand in Lockeport, was once featured on the Canadian $50 bill.

THE "REAL" CAPE ISLAND

Cape Sable Island, near Barrington Passage, is the home of the famous Cape Island boat first built by Ephraim Atkinson at Clark's Harbour in 1907. A typical Cape Islander is 11.5-m long with a 3.5-m beam. It draws little water, sitting on top of the water, and is used mostly in the lobster fishery.

THE HAWK

Living up to its name, The Hawk, on Cape Sable Island, is one
the prime bird-watching destinations in North America.

FRENCH FIRST

The French-speaking communities of West Pubnico, Middle West Pubnico and Lower West Pubnico were settled in 1653 by Acadians. The villages make up the oldest Acadian settlement in the world.

PAUL'S YARMOUTH RIDE

The famous American Revolutionary war hero, Paul Revere, was admitted as a Mason to the Freemasons in a lodge in Yarmouth County, and took his degree in Freemasonry near Yarmouth around 1772.

THE DEVIL'S IN THE DETAILS

In Nova Scotia it is said people built the front of their houses identical to the back so that the Devil wouldn't know which end was the front and could not enter.

GET OUT

In Nova Scotia, early homebuilders placed a shoe or boot in the wall next to the front door in order to kick out the Devil or evil spirits.

THE LUNENBURG
BUMP

One of the most distinctive architectural features in Canada is known as "The Lunenburg Bump." It can be found on many of the older houses in Lunenburg. In essence, the bump is an enlarged dormer extended out over the eaves. It can either be five-sided or rectangular. Most of the bumps are situated in the centre of the front and usually over the entrance.

LAND AHOY!

..360...361...
..362...

Legend has it that
there are 365 islands in
Mahone Bay, one for
each day of the year.

THE WHIRLIGIG

Shelburne is home to Canada's only whirligig and weather vane festival. Not surprisingly, the word "whirligig" comes from the verb "to whirl" and has been applied to toys dating back centuries. There's even mention of a whirligig affixed to a London tavern back in the 11th century.

WITH DISTINCTION

Dr. Daurene Lewis of Halifax, a seventh generation descendant of black slaves who settled in Annapolis Royal in 1783, became the first black woman mayor in North America when she was elected mayor of Annapolis Royal in 1984. In 1988, she became the first black woman in Nova Scotia to run (albeit unsuccessfully) in a provincial election. She has received numerous awards for her community service including the Order of Canada.

NORTH
OF FLORIDA

Annapolis Royal was settled in 1605 by Samuel de Champlain
and Pierre Du Gua de Monts. It is the oldest continuous
European settlement north of St. Augustine, Florida. Port
Royal was retained by France during most of the 17th Century
but was subject to frequent capture by the British. Then,
by recapture or treaty negotiations, it would be returned to
France. In 1713, the Treaty of Utrecht returned Port Royal to
the British for the last time. Annapolis Royal was the capital
of Nova Scotia from 1710 until the founding of Halifax
in 1749.

BIRDS OF PREY

Adopted as the provincial bird of Nova Scotia in 1994 by an Act of the House of Assembly, the Osprey is a bird of prey, sized between the larger eagle and the smaller hawk. Their main source of food is salt-water or fresh-water fish, depending on where they roost and hunt. They can often be seen hovering above the ocean, rivers and lakes looking for a meal. Then, in a spectacular display of aerobatics, they dive feet-first, skimming the water's surface, and then rise majestically into the air with a fish clasped in their talons.

A TOWERING SYMBOL

Adopted as the provincial tree by an Act of the House of Assembly in 1988, the Red Spruce represents the strength and resiliency of Nova Scotians. Able to survive in virtually any terrain and condition, the Red Spruce is the anchor of Nova Scotia's economy and is the province's number one lumber product. During early settlement, the twigs of the Red Spruce were brewed into a tea, which made an effective cure for scurvy. It has been a staple of the shipbuilding industry for centuries.

IN
THE
BLUE

Adopted as the provincial berry in January 1996, the Wild Blueberry is native to Nova Scotia — one of the five regions in Canada in which the berries grow naturally. Originally hand-picked in the wild, the blueberry is now cultivated throughout Nova Scotia and harvested by machines. Once popular primarily as market fare, the blueberries are now grown, frozen and exported to a number of countries around the world.

WHAT A BEAUTY!

* Apple may not be to scale

On August 31, 1922, The *Berwick Register* reported a three-pound "Rome Beauty" apple, the largest apple ever grown on record.

THE SHIPPING MAGNATE

Did you know that shipping magnate Sir Samuel Cunard was born November 21, 1787 in Halifax? The son of a master carpenter and timber merchant who had fled the American Revolution and settled in Halifax, Samuel founded the Cunard Line in 1840.

THE GROCERY KING

The grocery store conglomerate known today as Sobeys was founded in Stellarton by John W. Sobey in 1907 as a meat delivery business. In 1924, his son Frank H. Sobey, convinced him to expand into a full grocery business, serving Pictou County. From that point until his death, Frank was the driving force behind the business. Sobeys opened its first self-serve supermarket in 1949 and the chain eventually expanded throughout Atlantic Canada. During most of the second half of the 20th century, it was the region's dominant grocer.

THE WHOLE WORLD'S A STAGE

During the early days of settlement, the province's Annapolis
Basin region served as the cradle for both French and English
language theatre of Canada. Théatre de Neptune was the first
European theatre production in North America. English theatre
in Canada also started at Annapolis Royal. The tradition at
Fort Anne was to produce a play in honour of the Prince of
Wales's birthday. George Farquhar's *The Recruiting Officer*
was produced on January 20, 1733, by the officers of the
garrison to mark the Prince's birthday.

AT THE MOVIES

The Astor Theatre in Liverpool is the oldest performing arts venue in Nova Scotia. Built in 1902 as part of the historic town hall, the theatre was known as the Liverpool Opera House. Its stage hosted touring and local shows until 1917, when silent films were introduced. Gradually, the film presentation gained in frequency and popularity. In 1930, talking pictures were shown for the first time. At the same time the name was changed to the Astor Theatre after a theatre in New York. Today, the Astor is the oldest operating movie theatre in Canada. Until 2014, when it converted to a digital video and audio system, it used 35 millimetre film reels.

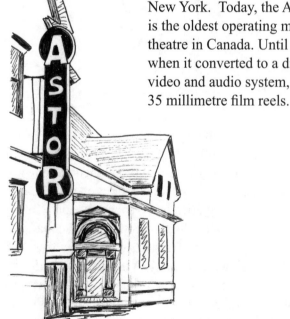

THERE'S GOLD IN THEM THAR HILLS!

While the world remembers the great Klondike gold rush that started in 1896, the truth is that gold was discovered in Nova Scotia several years earlier. Some researchers say the gold found here comes from a geological outcrop of Africa, left behind when North America and Africa split apart 160 million years ago. Gold was first discovered in Nova Scotia in 1858 at Mooseland on the Tangier River, inland from the Eastern Shore of Halifax County. A British army officer, Captain Champagne L'Estrange of the Royal Artillery, made the discovery while out for a day of moose hunting with a Mi'kmaq guide named Joe Paul.

READ A BOOK

The first public library in Nova Scotia formed in Yarmouth in January 1822. It was then known as the Yarmouth Book Society.

A DUBIOUS DISTINCTION

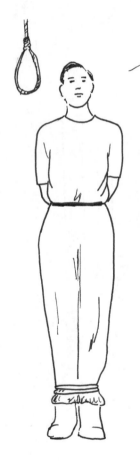

GOOD BYE, BOYS!

Everett Farmer, a 35-year-old construction labourer, has the unenviable distinction of being the last person hanged in Nova Scotia. His execution took place on December 14, 1937 in the Shelburne courthouse after he was tried and found guilty in the murder of his half-brother, Zachariah. According to public record, Farmer shot his half-brother during an argument while drinking home brew in his kitchen. He claimed it was self-defense. Ironically the victim had been tried and acquitted for the shooting murder of a cousin in 1919. Reportedly, Farmer's last words were, "Good bye boys."

A MOVIE LEGEND

A live deer filmed and photographed in Shelburne County was actually the inspiration for Disney animators working on the 1942 film classic, *Bambi*. An American, Dr. Jack Loré, shot the footage and photos. When he was a boy, the Loré family spent summers in Clyde River, Shelburne County, where naturalist Cecil Griffith, known locally as "Laddie," befriended the actual deer. Coincidentally the deer was called Bimbo. Eventually, the images ended up in the hands of Disney animators and the rest is movie history.

WE'RE BANKING ON IT

On September 3, 1825, businessman Enos Collins founded the Halifax Banking Company with Samuel Cunard and five others. It was called the Collins Bank. However, the first chartered bank in Nova Scotia opened on August 29, 1832, when the first branch of The Bank of Nova Scotia opened for business in Halifax at the corner of Granville and Duke streets. The bank's second branch opened seven years later in Yarmouth, but its real claim to fame is that it is said to have been the site of the first recorded bank robbery in North America in 1861.

CHEERS!

On July 17, 1749, Governor Cornwallis granted a license to sell beer and liquor to John Shippey, making it the first liquor license to be issued in New Scotland (Nova Scotia). Shippey named his tavern The Spread Eagle, as its sign was taken from the German coat of arms — The Double Eagle. Shortly after opening, the tavern became affectionately known as The Split Crow.

The Split Crow, located at the southwest corner of Salter and Water Street, quickly became a second home for sailors, mariners and travellers. It was there that they could expect comfortable lodgings, hearty platters of food and generous mugs of grog. In the tradition of the day, music was played, ladies entertained, politics were discussed and, inevitably, fights broke out. One of these fights resulted in the first ever murder charge in Nova Scotia.

LIGHTING THE WAY

The Sambro Island Lighthouse is the oldest lighthouse in Nova Scotia. In fact, built in 1758, it is the oldest continuously working lighthouse in the Americas. The tower height is 82 feet and it stands 140 feet above sea level. The lighthouse was built during the Seven Years War by the very first act passed by Nova Scotia's House of Assembly on October 2, 1758, which placed a tax on incoming vessels and alcohol imports to pay for the lighthouse. Located at the entrance to Halifax Harbour, the Sambro Light has been upgraded over the years, but predates New Jersey's Sandy Hook Light by four years, and Virginia's Cape Henry Light, Maine's photogenic Portland Head Light and Long Island's Montauk Point Light by three decades.

LET THE GAMES BEGIN

The Town of Antigonish is famous for two things. It is home to St. Francis Xavier University and the oldest continuous Highland Games outside of Scotland. Highland games are events held throughout the year in Scotland and other countries as a way of celebrating Scottish and Celtic culture and heritage, especially that of the Scottish Highlands. Certain aspects of the games are so well known as to have become emblematic of Scotland, such as the bagpipes, the kilt and the heavy events, especially the caber toss. While centred on competitions in piping and drumming, dancing, and Scottish heavy athletics, the games also include entertainment and exhibits related to other aspects of Scottish and Gaelic culture.

GOOD FOOD AND GOOD TIMES

The Order of Good Cheer was established by Samuel de Champlain in Port Royal (then known as Acadia) in the winter of 1606-07. It was the first gastronomic society in North America. The Order of Good Cheer provided good food and good times for the men to improve their health and morale during the long winter. Although it lasted only one winter, the society was a great success.

ROAD TRIP

On August 27, 1912, Thomas Wilby and Jack Haney left Halifax on the first ever cross-Canada motor trip. The excursion became known as the trip of the All-Red Route Reo.

THE HALFWAY POINT

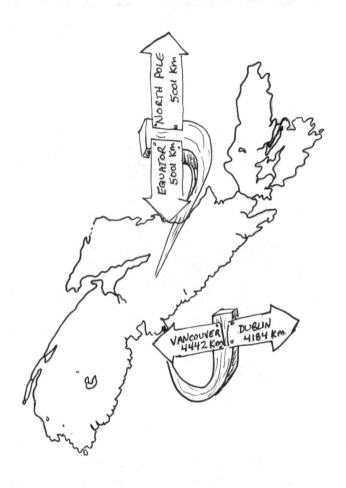

Did you know that Stewiacke is halfway between the Equator and the North Pole, or that Halifax is closer to Dublin, Ireland than it is to Victoria, British Columbia?

PARKLAND

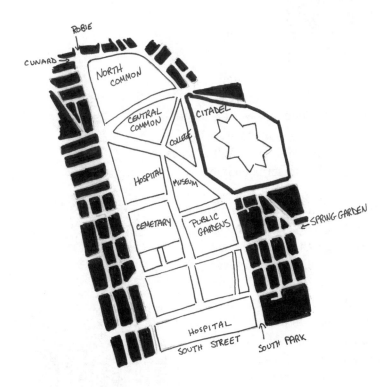

The Halifax Common, or the Commons as most people call the area in Halifax, is Canada's oldest urban park, with the North Common and the Central Common still in use as a public park area.

NOW THAT'S OLD!

The oldest tree ever found in Nova Scotia — a 418-year-old eastern hemlock — was discovered by a university student studying environmental science. While its exact location has never been publicly revealed, to protect the tree, it is known that it stands somewhere in southwestern Nova Scotia. With 418 rings, the hemlock beat the previous record in Nova Scotia by 20 years. The eastern hemlock, like many of the oldest trees in the world ever found, was not very large. Despite its age — the 11th-oldest eastern hemlock in the world — the tree is only 30 centimetres in diameter. It is the third oldest ever found in Canada. The two older eastern hemlock trees were both located in southern Ontario.

CANADA'S GAME

The Town of Windsor has long been a popular and important destination in the province, but it is its status as the birthplace of hockey that has put this Annapolis Valley town on the world map.

CAN YOU GET THAT, PLEASE?

Today, most people take their telephone for granted, but did you know this game-changing invention traces its roots back to Nova Scotia and the great mind of Alexander Graham Bell? The Scottish-born Bell obtained the patent for a multiple telegraph unit in 1875, and by 1876, when Bell was 29, the telephone was born. A year after that, the Bell Telephone Company formed.

Following his successful invention of the telephone and being relatively wealthy, Bell acquired land near Baddeck on Cape Breton Island in 1885. He established a summer estate complete with research laboratories, working with deaf people — including Helen Keller — and continued to invent. Baddeck would be the site of his experiments with hydrofoil technologies as well as the Aerial Experiment Association, which saw the first powered flight in Canada and the entire British Empire when the AEA Silver Dart flew off from the ice-covered waters of Bras d'Or Lake in 1909. Over his lifetime, Bell patented 18 inventions of his own, as well as 12 with colleagues.

The Bell family vacation home at Beinn Bhreagh is located near Baddeck on Cape Breton Island and eventually became Bell's final resting place. He died there on August 2, 1922.

SLOW DOWN!

Beeeeeeeeeeeeeep

The Town of Digby became the first jurisdiction in Nova Scotia to impose a speeding limit when, on July 29, 1910, it was decreed that, "No automobile shall be driven through the streets of the Town of Digby at a speed exceeding six miles per hour [10 km/h] and the drivers of automobiles shall keep the horn sounding while approaching and passing any person driving, walking or standing upon the streets. The penalty for a violation is $30 or sixty days in jail."

THE REAL SCARFACE

It is reputed that famed American gangster Al Capone, who was also known as Scarface, was a regular visitor to Riverport, a small fishing village on the province's South Shore, during the era of prohibition where he was said to hole up at the former Myrtle Hotel. Given the secluded location, and the fact that the area was heavily immersed in rum running, the legend seems very likely to be true.

MOVE
OVER!

At 2 a.m. on Sunday, April 15, 1923, the "rule of the road" changed in Nova Scotia. After that date, all traffic moved to the right-hand side of the road. Previously, automobiles, streetcars, horses, bicyclists, and all other vehicles and travellers adhered to the left-hand side of the road.

OUR VERY OWN TREASURE ISLAND

Oak Island, which is located just off the coast near Western Shore, Lunenburg County has attracted treasure seekers from around the world for centuries. The mystique that surrounds Oak Island dates back to 1795, when the hunt for the elusive treasure began. Theories abound as to what is buried beneath the rocky, coarse soil of this small island, which has spawned dozens of books and countless ghost stories. Many men have lost their fortunes and their lives trying to solve the clues and unlock the treasure vault, but to date, the island has refused to give up its secret.

Perhaps the most popular theory is that the treasure is a rich booty buried there by a band of bloodthirsty pirates — most notably Captain Kidd, who plied the waters of the Atlantic Ocean hundreds of years ago. Other theories suggest the stash is ancient Incan treasure, or the lost manuscripts of William Shakespeare. Some even theorize that the treasure is the Arc of the Covenant, hidden there by the Knights Templar, who were known to have visited the New World long before other early European explorers. The theories are only as limited as one's imagination.

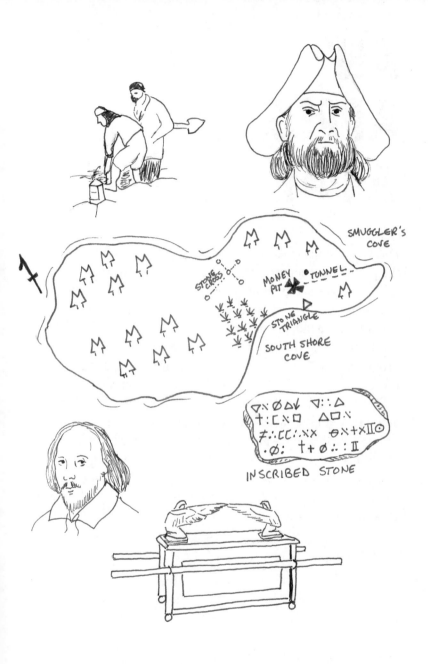

SMUGGLER'S
COVE

STONE
CROSS

MONEY
PIT

TUNNEL

STONE
TRIANGLE

SOUTH SHORE
COVE

INSCRIBED STONE

159

AN APPLE A DAY

Did you know apples contribute more than $50 million to the provincial economy? Nova Scotia currently produces an annual average of approximately 2.35 million bushels of apples, which is equal to between eight and nine per cent of the Canadian production or one per cent of the U.S. production. Today, the Annapolis Valley is the centre of apple production on Canada's Eastern Seaboard. Records show the presence of apples in Port Royal in 1610 and at LaHave in 1635. It was reported that 1,584 apple trees were distributed among 54 families at Port Royal. It also shows an orchard of improved varieties planted in 1635 by Pierre Martin at Belleisle, Annapolis County. The first export of apples in Nova Scotia is believed to have been made in 1849 by Benjamin Weir of Halifax and Ambrose Bent of Paradise, who exported them from Halifax to Liverpool, England.

WOULD YOU LIKE SOME CHEESE WITH THAT?

Situated in one of the cooler climate limits for vines, Nova Scotia has had a long and rich tradition for growing grapes for wine dating back to the early 1600s. It's actually quite possible this was one of the first areas to cultivate grapes in North America.

The history of growing grapes in Nova Scotia goes back to 1611. That's when French settler Louis Herbert first planted a small vineyard in Bear River. Nova Scotia's first commercial vintage started in 1980 and years later, a Nova Scotia wine, Jost's 1999 Vidal Ice Wine, took home Canada's Wine of the Year Award.

Nova Scotia wineries have differentiated themselves into several very distinct regions including Northumberland Strait, the Annapolis Valley, Malagash Peninsula and the LaHave River Valley.

SEASONAL FAVOURITE

The classic Christmas song, "It's Beginning to Look a Lot Like Christmas" was written in 1951 by American composer and songwriter, Meredith Willson. Originally titled "It's Beginning to Look Like Christmas," the song has been recorded by many artists, but was first a hit for Perry Como. Bing Crosby recorded a version on October 1, 1951, which is still widely played today. According to local legend, Willson wrote the song while visiting Nova Scotia and staying in Yarmouth's Grand Hotel. The song makes reference to a "tree in the Grand Hotel, one in the park as well..."; the park being Frost Park, directly across the road from the Grand Hotel, which still operates in a newer building on the same site as the old hotel.

VERNON OICKLE is an international award winning journalist, editor and writer with almost 35 years working in newspapers. He is the author of 23 books, including *Ghost Stories of Nova Scotia*, the bestselling *Crow* series and the *Nova Scotia Outstanding Outhouse Reader*. Vernon and his wife Nancy have two sons, Kellen and Colby. He continues to reside in Liverpool where he was born and raised.

JULIE ANNE BABIN grew up in Liverpool. She earned her Bachelor of Arts from Dalhousie University and her Bachelor of Fine Arts from the Nova Scotia College of Art and Design (NSCAD). Julie then returned to her hometown to establish ADJA Studio and Gallery. In 2014, she became proprietor of the Welcome Matte Frame Shoppe, adding custom framing to her resume. Currently, Julie resides in Liverpool producing her own work while raising her three sons, Caius, Asa and Desmond.